Beyond the Veil

Monica L. Sanders

Beyond the Veil and Study Guide

To order additional copies, contact:

A LOTT of Sista Love
P.O. Box 481244
Charlotte, North Carolina 28269
www.alottofsistalove.org

BEYOND THE VEIL

Matthew 27:51-53 (New King James Version)

"Then, behold, the veil of the temple was torn in two from top to bottom; and the earth quaked, and the rocks were split, and the graves were opened; and many bodies of the saints who had fallen asleep were raised; and coming out of the graves after His resurrection, they went into the holy city and appeared to many."

Foreword

Beyond the Veil is from the A LOTT of Sista Love monthly newsletter, which is meant to awaken those things that are asleep, dead, or buried deep inside us that hinder us from going beyond the veil. It is meant to bring hope to its readers and help them to anchor themselves and to enter into the presence of the LORD in their daily walk – to seek GOD for what we can be in HIM.

As you read this book, take time to answer the questions asked in Moments of Reflection. They will help you examine yourself. Open your hearts so you may regain or set your spiritual life in order and become steadfast and sure of your call. *Beyond the Veil* is a tool to return us to God's ordained Word through one of His servants. It is meant to catch the vision of the extraordinary life that God has for you and to show you the way to move toward that vision.

Beyond the Veil was named during its birth by Pamela Mullins, former Advisory Board member of A LOTT of Sista Love (ALOSL). ALOSL is a women's empowerment group. For more information, visit our Web site www. alottofsistalove.org

-Monica L. Sanders, MSA, CHRM, C.Min

This book is dedicated to my Naomi's

Clara Ella Griffin, my GRAMMY! WOW, what a powerful women. She was not your ordinary GRANDMOTHER. She was anointed in her own way...she loved God but was not religious. Go figure. She loved me unconditionally and was my best friend. She was able to restore me and rebuke me as no one else could and I could not get angry with her. The more I was around her, the more I wanted to be around her and we could spend hours together without saying a word.

Gerri Vitulano, my first supervisor! She taught me how to survive in the workplace. A small Italian woman with a BIG spirit, she wanted the best for me -- my own desk, computer, telephone, and responsibilities – even though I only worked for her for eight weeks during one summer.

Karen Gaskins Jones, a tall, anointed, professional DIVA! She took charge like an Army Colonel. Her presence was, and still is, powerful, especially in a room full of male colleagues. She never wavered or was intimidated, and I loved to see her in action. She proved to me that I could hold my own without sacrificing my femininity. She taught me how to share with others, especially when God was blessing me. And she introduced me to another beautiful woman, Maureen Delaney, who showed me that I could be thoughtful as well as tough!

Stephanie V. Lott, friend and fighter! My best girlfriend for almost 25 years, she never missed a beat with me. She was always there, with a canoe, to support me when I stepped out to walk on water – just in case. She loved my family as much as I do and also had a close relationship with my husband and children.

Pastor Jo Ann Browning, Ebenezer A.M.E. Church (Fort Washington, Maryland)! A Mighty Warrior for God, she was my co-pastor for 12 years and taught me from the pulpit. From her I learned how to be in covenant with my husband and to love him wholeheartedly. She taught me how to dress as a Christian Woman without dressing like a Nun. She has a flair that you just want to mimic. She taught me how to kneel before the Lord and still cross my feet.

These five women were and continue to be my grace in times of stress and need. Not many women have truly inspired me in my life, but these women not only had time for me but commanded my full attention. They taught me the valuable lesson that inspiration comes from others as well as from within – a lesson we should all remember.

I thank these wonderful women, you, and God for this opportunity to share the lessons I have learned in my life. And I take this opportunity to shout out to my mom, Claretha Basil, for always wanting the best for me.

Sista Monica L. Sanders, MSA, CHRM, C.Min, and Founder, A LOTT of Sista Love.

About the Author

Monica L. Sanders is a God-fearing, prayer warrior for GOD. A native of Washington, DC, she relocated to Charlotte, North Carolina, in August 2005. She is the CEO of Kingdom Consulting, a human resources firm. Sista Monica, as she is called, is a Leader and Visionary for Today's times and knows how to turn pain into power. She is the founder of A LOTT of Sista Love (named in memory of her dear friend and confidant, the late Stephanie V. Lott), a non-profit women's empowerment organization. She has also formed many programs under the umbrella of Kingdom Development, including Girlz@TheGate, Bent Not Broken, and Sassy Singles. Her most rewarding endeavor is W.O.W. (Women of Wisdom), a program that mentors young girls, ages 10-17. W.O.W has become a particular passion because of the need to enrich the lives of young ladies to help them toward a healthier future.

Sista Monica formed a basketball team for boys under 11 in collaboration with her husband. The team, the University City All-Stars, competed in their first tournament last summer in Wilmington, North Carolina. They took third place.

She earned a B.A. in Communications from Trinity College, Washington, D.C., a masters in Administration and Human Resources from Central Michigan University, Mount Pleasant, Michigan, and a certification in Ministry from Kingdom University, which is under the leadership of Dr. Cindy Trimm. She has also done coursework in theological studies at Hood Theological Seminary, Salisbury, North Carolina, and will return in the spring for additional study. She is one whose hugs can discern and cure at the same time. She is truly an anointed individual and has a heartfelt concern for others.

She was one of the featured **new** authors at the Charlotte, North Carolina, Literary Festival.

God has given Sista Monica a TRUE passion to empower women to reach their full potential, to make their dreams a reality, and to celebrate life with one another to God's fullest. She keeps to this assignment from Him, no matter what!

TABLE OF CONTENTS

What Are You Afraid Or Fearful Of?

Fear is an emotional response to threats and danger. Fear should be distinguished from anxiety, which typically occurs without any external threat. Fear is related to the specific behaviors of escape and avoidance; anxiety is the result of threats perceived to be uncontrollable or unavoidable. Fear is often connected to pain (e.g. some fear heights because they fear falling and suffering severe injury or death). Psychologists John B. Watson and Paul Ekman have suggested that fear is one of several basic, innate emotions (e.g. joy and anger). Fear is a survival mechanism and usually occurs in response to a specific negative stimulus. (Source: http://en.wikipedia.org/wiki/Fear)

Fear is one of the tools the enemy uses. We are afraid of making mistakes, afraid of trusting in faith, afraid of what people will say, afraid of going back to school, afraid of having a too-long-overdue conversation with someone we love or care about. And sometimes we are just afraid of actually being successful.

Our fears hold us back from becoming all that God has ordained for us to be. Are we in fear or just fearful? There is a difference. Fear is an emotional response; being fearful is a worrying temperament. There are four Scriptures in the Bible about being fearful and 52 Scriptures related to fear. Fear holds us captive; it is a stronghold that may allow us to be safe in the world but will keep us from being bold in the Lord. 2 Corinthians 10:4-5, "For the weapons of our warfare are not carnal but mighty in God for pulling down strongholds, casting down arguments and every high thing that exalts itself against the knowledge of God, bringing every thought into captivity to the obedience of Christ."

What are you afraid or fearful of...success, failure, going back to school, commitment, relationships, making mistakes, looking silly, being judged, being right or wrong, being criticized, failing to what God wants you to do.

What is God's plan for your life? Are you afraid to fulfill it? Remember, when you are afraid you stop progress.

Moments of Reflection

Take a moment to list the things you are afraid of – the things that keep you from moving forward.

Beside each listed item, write why you are afraid to conquer your fears in that particular area.

Finally, list the steps you can take to conquer your fears and move pass them.

What Do You Think Of When You Hear "Friendly Fire"?

God woke me one September morning and led me to think of a new weapon in the enemy's arsenal…friendly fire. *Wikipedia* defines friendly fire as a term originally adopted by the United States military to refer to **fire from one's own side or allied forces and not fire from enemy forces**.

But friendly fire can also describe friends who can be used by the enemy to accidentally hurt or destroy you, regardless of how much they love you – like Peter and Jesus (colleagues), or Paul (associate) in Acts 16:16-23. (*The Rules of Engagement: Satanic Weapons Exposed*, Vol. III) I also found that the term is used in many video games to describe a setting in which players on the same team can damage and kill each other.

In other words, friendly fire can be a betrayal by someone you thought had your best interest at heart, but IS instead a person who Satan uses as a weapon against you.

Friendly fire can come from anyone, even:

- ➤ Sista friend
- ➤ Family member (sister, brother, mother, spouse, etc.)
- ➤ Ministerial colleagues
- ➤ Mentors
- ➤ Associates
- ➤ Confidants
- ➤ Business Partner(s)
- ➤ Counselors

In 2008 my year of new beginnings, I found myself facing friendly fire too many times. As I searched for ways to avoid or cope with this menace, I found that, for me, the best counsel was that offered by life coach and best selling author Dr. N. Cindy Trimm, an anointed, dynamic servant of God and visionary, www.cindytrimm.com.

My strong counsel to you today would be to take nothing and no one for granted. The ones we love, and the ones that love us, could very well be used to provoke us into the forfeiture of divine opportunities, ministries, and ultimately the fulfillment of purpose, maximization of potential, and reaching our destiny. One of the reasons why I believe this particular strategy is so powerful is that we are usually more relaxed around people with whom we are close so we let our hair down, so to speak.

Friendly fire is real. Pay close attention to this satanic weapon and expose it for what it is! Don't spend time on things that hold you back or as expressed in Tye Tribbett's Gospel album "We are in a war y'all and it is time to STAND UP!"

Moments of Reflection

Have you been ambushed by friendly fire lately?

What did you do?

How did you handle the situation? Or did it resolve itself?

Want vs. Need

Psalms 23:1 *The LORD is my Shepherd; I shall not want.* This is a familiar scripture to many Christians, seasoned or not. But do we really know what this passage means?

Read this scripture again and mediate on it and I believe you'll find it should be our anthem in these uncertain times, particularly in the current economic climate If the Lord is our shepherd we have everything we need and will truly not want for anything as long as we trust in God's will. It may be that what we want and pray for is not God's will for us. Perhaps we have not been good stewards over the gifts He has given us. Have we been like Miriam (Moses and Aaron's sister) and have a murmuring spirit? Too often we believe what God gives us is not enough. Instead of rejoicing in the gifts we have, we try to exceed ourselves and constantly ask for more. When is enough, enough? When will our wanting align with our needs? Let's take a moment to examine the difference between a want and a need.

Dictionary.com defines a **want** as:
> ➢ To feel a need or a desire for; wish for; *to want one's dinner; always wanting something new*
> ➢ To wish, need, crave, demand, or desire

A **need**, according to Dictionary.com is:
> ➢ A requirement, necessary duty, or obligation
> ➢ A lack of something wanted or deemed necessary: *to fulfill the needs of the assignment*

Study these definitions to distinguish between them, then align yourself according to God's will for your life and not what you want God's will to be. Your *need* will always be more important to God than your *want*. All God wants is you! All you need is God! Take a moment to study Psalm 23; absorb it; accept it. Then be thankful that as long as you walk upright before God you will never lack.

Remember the word of God in Philippians 4:19, *—But my God shall supply all your needs according to His riches in glory in Christ Jesus*

Moments of Reflection

Describe what "want" means to you?

What do you want right now?

Does what you want align with your needs?

Does what you want reflect God's will?

Does your want overshadow your true need, the need that God will satisfy?

Stand and Stay: Hold Fast To Your Purpose During The Famine

The world around us is in a panic mode; the environment is ripe for chaos and violence. Children are mistreated; families are murdered and, most disturbing, racism on the rise again. Yet it seems we sit dormant – waiting for God – forgetting that we must stay steadfast in our purpose until change comes. So many of us are pregnant with possibilities and it is imperative that as disruptive forces surround us and things seem to crumble, we must *stand*. God's word stands forever and He proclaims His promises. (Isaiah 40:8).

What do we mean by stand?

When you *stand*, you decide to remain in the place that God has destined for you. Standing means you do not forego your purpose and destiny because of external considerations or conditions. These have nothing to do with your position in God.

How do we stand? We stand when we:

PRAY - Find time each day to seek God (2 Chronicles 7:14). Read the Word, find Scriptures that keep you focused, take a class to become closer to Him, and find others who can pray with you and encourage you in your standing moment.

PURPOSE - Seek God for purpose (James 1:5-7). Ask God to make you aware, to help you listen to Him, to understand what He has in mind for you.

POSITION - Live and Love according to God's Will (Deuteronomy 10:12-13). Continue to prepare yourself so when your change comes, you will be ready – in the right mind to accept it. Get your money, health, relationships, and mind right.

PRESS - Continue to seek God with vigor. (Hosea 6:33). Attend church, become involved with activities of empowerment; search for God's Will.

We are at a dawning of change: change in the White House, change in our households, change in our lives, change in our relationships and, most important, we are moving to our next level of change in God. We must *stand* to remain true to our promises and to fulfill our destiny toward God's promise. And we can begin by keeping Christ in Christmas this year – by standing in God's Promises. And that is truly going beyond the veil!

Moments of Reflection

Are you standing in the promises God has for you?

If yes, how are you standing?

If no, why not? What is making you waver? Why are you giving up on God?

Reflect on your gifts from God. When has there ever been a time that God did not stand up for you?

Servanthood*

Just as we are committed and consistent in how we spend money to satisfy our wants, we should be committed and consistent in our *servanthood* to God. God invites us to serve and we want to serve, but too often it is a commitment with questions and/or hidden refusals – as if we have choices. Who said we could hesitate to accept God's agenda? I believe God's intention is to stretch us in a challenging way – to force us to deviate from our customs and modus operandi. Too often it seems as if we want to control God, to determine what He would have us do or not do. Whose agenda are we on? I hope you don't think you are on your own agenda – LOL!!!

What if we woke up one morning and found that God had decided that because we had not been committed and consistent in our *servanthood*, he was going to not be committed and consistent with us. Where would that leave you? Would that leave you without a home, without a husband or significant other, with a sick child? Would you find yourself with no food, no transportation, no speech, no sight, no friends or family to love you? Would you have an illness beyond recovery and face death or just bad grades? What would you face? You fill in the blanks.

Our response to serving has too often been misguided. We are to respond according to God's awaiting request and not our waiting request. Our response to serving should be in a posture of humble obedience and it should be made as quickly as possible. When our response is aligned with what God has called for us to be – when He brings forth the birth of Destiny and Purpose in our lives, then we truly do serve. In many ways our prayers are delayed because we continue to miss the mark; we continue to be open to everything but God. We stand in awe at the bling-bling of human society and ignore the grandeur of God.

In the Bible, Luke is my favorite disciple. Not only did he have sensitivity to women, he had the boldness to write about them. In Luke 1:38, he speaks of Mary, "And Mary said, Yes, I see it all now: I'm the Lord's maid, ready to serve. Let it be with me just as you say. Then the angel departed from her." (*The Message: The Bible In Contemporary Language*). Mary clearly knew what service to God meant – she gave birth to Jesus!!! What a task; she didn't know why she was chosen, she didn't know if David would stay with her, let alone support her in her commitment to God in the birth of Jesus.

Yet she responded in a posture of humble obedience. She responded as quickly as possible. I truly know serving God sometimes can be fearful and confusing, but I also truly know God will give you strength to follow each instruction and direction He gives. When you are challenged and confused, He will give you courage to *Press In and Press On*. His promises for you are so grand you may not even comprehend them, He sees as we cannot see...even with thick glasses. Seek God! Ask Him to give you patience so you may be *committed and consistent* in 2009 and beyond. ALOSL needs you and God has called you; hear God calling you. Don't be too busy for God and miss what He truly has for you. He does not have to choose us, but I am so thankful that He does!

*Although you will not find *servanthood* in the dictionary, I coined the word to reflect our role of service to God and how we should respond to His call.

Moments of Reflection

How are you serving God?

To what are you being *committed and consistent* to in your *servanthood*?

Is it hard for you to serve? Why or why not?

Are You Dealing In Illusions/Magic/Tricks?

Your quick response may be --NO WAY! You might be offended that I even asked the question and demand an explanation. Well here it goes... Illusions/Magic/Tricks are funny things. According to Wikipedia, *Magic is a performing art that entertains an audience by creating illusions of seemingly impossible or supernatural feats, using purely natural means. These feats are called magic tricks, effects or illusions.*

As we know, one who performs such illusions is called a magician. Some magicians may also be referred to by names reflecting the type of magical effects they present: prestidigitators, conjurors, illusionists, mentalists, escape artists, and ventriloquists. We may not do tricks as defined in Wikipedia, but we do use illusions and magic tricks in our lives and in how we relate to the lives of others.

Do you show people only one side of you, hiding the other? Do you portray one side in public – another in private, still another at work or with friends. Do you have a different illusion or trick for each aspect of your life? Are you real with what is going on in your life or do you perform as if you were an actor in a play or movie called LIFE? Are you embarrassed that you cannot be real and express your true needs or even just be accountable to yourself? Perhaps if we explore the kind of performer you are, it will be helpful.

***Prestidigitator* --** Do you try to make something from nothing and invent roadblocks to keep people at a distance? Or do you use a spate of words, balancing them in the air simultaneously, to confuse others and discourage meaningful communication?

Conjuror -- Do you put up a smoke screen when people are close to you – or getting close to you – so they can't discover your real secret or learn what you are really about? Do you invent an illusion that you want to do better and be better – but then continue to do the same old thing?

Illusionist – Do you distort the reality that you share with other people? Do you have your own reality, one that only makes sense to you? Do you believe everybody is wrong and you are always right? Have you ever taken a self-check?

Mentalist – Do you proclaim that you know what others are thinking even before you have heard them out? Do you assume to know what things and situations are, even though most of the time you have misjudged the events? Do you profess and pray for healthy relationships, even though you cannot handle such a relationship because you are accustomed to unhealthy ones – ones that tear you down instead of building you up?

Escape artist – Do you try to divert attention from an unpleasant reality? Perhaps you disappear and make excuses for not returning to what God has charged you with? Do you act as if you care, but as soon as you get a chance run from your calling or assignment? Do you act as if your name was Forest Gump?

Ventriloquist – Do you equivocate -- think one thing and say another? Do your actions match your words? Do you pretend to be sound and tell others "I am blessed and highly favored!" Do you spend more time complaining to God then praising and worshipping Him?

James 5:16 (*The Message: The Bible In Contemporary Language*) states *Make this your common practice: Confess your sins to each other and pray for each other so that you can live together whole and healed. The prayer of a person living right with God is something powerful to be reckoned with.* Let's make things happen. Let's not do magic tricks or continue to create illusions. God is watching and He is not amused by performances of deceit and/or cleverness. We should all remember…"Silly Rabbit, Tricks (Trix) are for Kids!"

Monica L. Sanders

Moments of Reflection

What tricks are you performing?

Will you continue to dabble in magic or will you confess and let others know who you really are? And if that reality is not what God would have you be, will you let His power, through others, help you?

Commitment

Commitment according to Dictionary.com is "The act of committing, pledging, or engaging oneself." Engaging one's self – what a great way to think of commitment. Take a moment and see if you are engaging yourself. I often struggle and wonder whether people are committing themselves to anything, be it faith, family, friends, careers, community, etc.

And when I reflect on our commitment to each other, my perspective is that commitment is lacking. How often do we wonder why we are not happy or comfortable with ourselves? We know there is something missing; we think if we ignore it, the feeling will go away. But ignoring the feeling doesn't work. What will work is engaging ourselves – making a commitment.

So let's make a commitment now as we are reading this book that *It Is Time*. It is time to come together and be committed to something other than our own desires or accomplishments.

Moments of Reflection

Ask yourself: What am I committed to?

Better still, ask: In what direction am I engaging myself?

Accountability

Accountability can be a heavy word for some of us!

When you look up accountability in a thesaurus, you find it means: responsibility, liability, and answerability. If you delve further into the meaning of these words and allow your mind to ponder those meanings, your thoughts might go something like the following:

Responsibility – that equates to dependability. When we miss the mark (we're not responsible), we might look for someone to blame. That transitions us to liability, which in essence carries the meaning of danger. And this path guides us to answerability. Then before we know it, we're back to where we started – at accountability.

Does this sound confusing? Maybe that's why whenever we think or consider accountability it can become too difficult for us to deal with directly. We try to run away from it and avoid it in our daily lives. A friend, during a discussion on accountability, once told me: *We should not waste our time on others who don't appreciate who we are or who won't choose to do better.*

At first, I was baffled by this response. Initially I thought it was selfish. My friend expounded upon this revelation by saying: *There are many others waiting in line to experience you and what God has for them through you.* WOW! I never thought of it in that way. Since then, my friend and I have drifted apart. Now I sometimes wonder if that friend was one of those persons for whom accountability, at the level I was projecting, appeared to be too much.

It is time to be accountable not only to yourself, but also to those others who require it of you. Think about it, pray, and take that step. We truly need each other to make this thing called *Life* work! We truly need to be accountable.

Moments of Reflection

Is accountability too hard?

If so, why?

Make a list of what you have been accountable for in your life.

How does your list compare to that of others who have been accountable to you?

How does that make you feel?

Your response

As we move forward as God has ordained, it is imperative that we respond as Christians in these famine times. Our response must be careful and correct according to God's Will. We have to become the antidote for those who are seeking a healing. Our response should now be connected to our blessings and next level in God. Clearly these economic times are showing us that our past responses have devastated housing, finances, and relationships.

When I looked up the definition of *responding*, I found there are three derived forms of the word and several words that derive from the same word. Here are just a few: responder, response time, responsibility, responsible, and responsive. These are different words, yet they carry the same, heavy mantle of responding – to take action. This may seem a little confusing, but a careful second reading will help you to understand the message. When we respond, we are the responder. When we respond, our response time is vital to those who sent out a request. Our responding not only makes us responsible, it gives us responsibility. Finally, once we have responded in a mature way we then will reap benefits from God for our God is responsive!

However, too often we fail to respond; we think others will do it for us. We think "they don't need my two cents' worth; there are enough people involved; they won't miss me." But did you ever think that your response to something might be someone else's release! What is keeping you from responding to the call to action in your life? Why do you ignore the call to bless others, the call to hear yourself, the call to connect to those who may help you through your trials and tribulations by praying and sharing their testimony with you? Too often our response or lack of response has been the cause of broken relationships, mistrust, mishaps, missed opportunities – and resulted in our faltering in our relationship with God.

Ask yourself, why is it so *hard* for us to respond – not only respond in a godly way, but also in a civil way? We don't RSVP; we don't call. It is easier to apologize or make excuses then to keep the commitment we made. We deal in our intention rather than in keeping our word. Intensions – there's another heavy word for me and perhaps for you. So often we truly have great intentions and expect God to know our true and pure heart because He has granted us life. (Proverbs 12:2, "A good man obtains favor from the Lord, but a man of wicked intentions He will condemn.)

But we must earn the Keys to the Kingdom. Intentions might position us to receive the Keys, but they do not guarantee that we will inherit the Kingdom. We cannot claim the Keys on someone else's promises. Yet that is what we attempt when we choose to sit and let others guess what we are going to do or not do by our lack of response. And doesn't that take us back to accountability?

Now you might ask, are there rules of responding?

Yes. I believe there are rules of responding – rules that have a godly perspective. For example:

- *Responding in love* -- Having the heart of God to show Agape Love

- *Responding honestly* – Having the grace of God

- *Responding prayerfully* – Having a prayer encounter with God

- *Responding without hidden agendas* – Having a godly mindset to do without expectations of any return

- *Responding out of the call of God* – Moving in God's Wall in your life and the lives of those around you.

Today, more than ever, God is watching our responses. The way we respond to the world and those in it is a test administered by God. If we pass, then He can trust us to move to our next level in Him. If we are not responding in prosperity and our finances are not sound in this time of famine, then we should check ourselves to make sure we are in agreement with God's plan for our lives. What the world is going through has nothing to do with us unless we were out of alignment (Proverbs 14:11). Take **time out** for playing, but be sure you allow **time in** for becoming and being! Aren't you tired of the same ole same ole by now? (1Timothy 4:12-16)

Get the word out. Teach all these things. And don't let anyone put you down because you're young. Teach believers through your life: by word, by demeanor, by love, by faith, by integrity. Stay at your post and read Scripture, give counsel, teach. And that special gift of ministry you were given when the leaders of the church laid hands on you and prayed – you want to always keep that dusted off and in use.

"Cultivate your gifts. Immerse yourself in them. And, let people see you mature right before their eyes! Keep a firm grasp on both your character and your teaching. Don't be diverted. Just keep at it. Both you and those who hear you will experience salvation." (*The Message: The Bible In Contemporary Language*)

Moments of Reflection

Where you in responding?

What makes responding so hard for you?

What steps will you take to improve how you respond in the future?

Are You a Great Pretender?

Are You A Great Pretender? Is the theme for your life, "Fake It Until I Make it!"? As a child, one of my brothers and I would pretend we were running a store. We set up our room as a store, labeled stuff, had a cash register and bags, and gave receipts – the whole nine yards. I always wanted to be the "choon-choon" lady (a cashier). We called her that because it was the sound registers in stores made.

I pretended to be a cashier. I rang up my brother's items, bagged them, and sent him on his way with a cheerful, "Sir, thank you for shopping with us, have a nice day, and do come again!" Of course there were times in our pretend play when he wanted to be the cashier and run the register. Then I would have a fit. Even in pretend play, I didn't want him to replace me in the role I loved so much.

So I'd threaten to quit – say "I am not playing anymore." Now doesn't that sound familiar? Even in our adult lives when people don't play as we choose, we quit. In my pretend play, my brother would always give in and let me go on pretending to be the best cashier ever. And that also sounds familiar to me because we still pretend in our everyday lives. Of course, as adults we pretend in different ways, even though we know grownups should not play childish games.

In our adult life we should not pretend to be:

  ♥ Listening when others speak and share
  ♥ Professional
  ♥ In love

♥ Concerned
♥ Okay with the way our life is going
♥ Over the divorce, hurt, pain, bitterness
♥ Caring mothers, daughters, aunties, Sista-girls
♥ Knowledgeable of things about which we have no clue
♥ Loving each other, unconditionally
♥ Happy
♥ Ready for our next level with God by professing – "God, we are available to you!"when we are not. Who are we to pretend and place God on hold?

(These actions should not be false. They should be real and true.)

I find that one of the most common pretenses for adults is the profession of their belief that God is the Head of their lives and will protect them. Then when an adversary comes, they run quickly for cover instead of facing the adversary secure in the protection of the Lord.

As adults we also pretend to create a lifestyle and begin to believe in it. We get sold on the status quo. We do not want to admit there are challenges, not only with the way we live but with the way we give. Go ahead; confess that when I mentioned *give*, you immediately thought of money. But giving should also be in your love, time, talent –

those things that you are not only purposed for but destined to do. God requires us to honor Him, draw near to Him, not just pretend (Matthew 15:8). He wants us to give Him our all, by our acts as well as our words. We can deceive others but He is the one truly knowing being and He is taking note. (Mark 7:6) God always requires our true selves. This requirement is why He gives us mercy, grace, and compassion daily. So don't just pretend to be one thing at work – or in life. Become it; get certified in all your endeavors and know that God will guide you through life.

By the way, my brother went on to be – and still – is the best retail manager in the Army/Air Force Exchange Services. He has received numerous awards and recognition for his service and achievement, including monetary awards, during his service in the United States and overseas. He once pretended to be a customer; God made him a high ranking government servant, serving military families.

Sometimes we pretend to one thing, but God makes us into something totally different. What are you pretending with your imaginary friends, your make-believe status, false expectations, and made-up stories? Stop pretending and seek God so He can guide your life and help you to become what He wants you to be and to do what He wants you to do.

Moments of Reflection

What are you pretending to be?

Is it working?

When the pretending is over, how do you feel?

Do you think God is pleased with your pretending? Reflect on how you appear to Him.

The Evaluation

SIX- MONTH EVALUATION! Did you get that promotion?

In my former life, I was a senior manager in Human Resources. Working with other managers, I set a standard for the six-month evaluations of employees. These evaluations helped us assess each other and also let us gauge how well we, and our employees, were meeting the standards for the annual evaluation.

These evaluations helped me avoid surprises or disgruntled employees at the yearly appraisal. Although the main objective of a performance evaluation meeting between employer and employee is to acknowledge how well employees are performing their jobs, the meetings can also provide the employer with an opportunity to help employees improve their performance.

During this time a manager or supervisor can see just how effectively an employee is working within a department and determine what, if anything, needs to be done to improve their effectiveness. These evaluations, which usually include many different aspects of job expectations, also provide employees with an opportunity to learn how effective they are and how they can improve their performance. Equally important is that it gives employees a chance to air any grievances or problems they have in relation to their job performance.

In the secular world, once an evaluation has been carried out the employee has the right to make written or oral comments about the evaluation findings. They may, if they wish, include information they feel is pertinent to their evaluation that has been omitted. Then all this information is placed in the employee's personnel file for future reference. Now ask yourself – in your last performance evaluation were you able to answer the questions honesty and clearly – as a good employee?

Now think for a moment about being an employee of God. How would He rate you in a six-month evaluation? Would you be able to voice or write comments to God in prayer? If you could, *Congratulations!* Then you are clearly walking in the way prescribed in Jeremiah 29:11, "For I know the plans I have for you, says the Lord. They are plans for good and not for disaster, to give you **a future** and a **hope.**" Be thankful you are moving in the right direction as it relates to your purpose in God. If you are favorably evaluated by God, you will receive not only a pay raise but also the bonuses He has promised you.

If you are not able to answer His questions or have not performed the duties God has laid out for you, then borrowing the words of Donald Trump in *The Apprentice* —You are FIRED!!!! And we would never want that. So thank God for His grace and the mercy He extends when He gives us second chances! Acknowledge and confess, "For all have sinned; all fall short of God's glorious standard." (Romans 3:23) Let's stop falling short. Let's get up and move toward what God has ordained for us so His evaluation of us will promote us higher in Him.

—From everyone who has been given much, much will be demanded; and from the one who has been entrusted with much, much more will be asked. Luke 12:48 NIV.

Moments of Reflection

Here are some questions to ponder for your evaluation discussion with God:

What does God's evaluation for the year look like (New Year's Resolutions as we call it)?

What does your Vision Board look like? Have you marked off or added anything? Did you even make one?

What are your strengths and weaknesses?

What are you doing to work toward a better life in God?

Are you abiding by the job description God has laid out for you?

Do you have you all the qualifications necessary to carry out the duties you been assigned?

Spiritual Death

This is not dealing with death in the earthly sense — a killer disease or fatal accident. Spiritual Death happens when our flesh battles with our spirit and the flesh wins.

Dr. Cindy Trimm of Cindy Timm Ministries, (www. cindytrimm.com) explains "Untimely death aborts destinies, executes purpose, and assassinates potential." Thus, we are always in jeopardy of spiritual death, especially when, as women, we deal with the cares of life. For example, when we marry and begin to let ourselves go. We become last because we are working and worrying about everything and everybody else until one day we look up and say:

Who Am I?

*Where Did the **Me** Go?*

Who Is this Person that I Have Become?

We can also ask those same questions about the process of spiritual death. We become so busy we forget what God has truly ordained for us. We encounter spiritual miscarriages, abortions, and suicidal thoughts. We never work through what God expects from us. We do not recognize who we *really* are in God. Instead, we turn the things of God into a "Chick Flick."

My husband loves violent movies with lots of stuff being blown up. His favorite movies are *Die Hard*, *Die Harder*, and *Die Hardest*. Whenever I want to watch a romantic movie, he calls it a "Chick Flick, basing that observation on the love, the crying, the emotional pouring out – enough is enough he would say. In many ways, that is how non-Christians view our walk with God. They think we are emotionally unstable; we are whiners who are never satisfied. They think we serve a wimpy God. But we know that cannot be true because Jesus performed surgery on death. He has taken the stinger out of death and His followers will never die spiritually (1 Corinthians. 15:55.) In Revelations 1:18 Jesus took the keys of hell and death, so why are we dying?

Why are *you* dying? Proverbs 18:21, *Death and life are in the power of the tongue*. What are you allowing to be on your tongue? Unforgiveness, Hatred, Shame, Disappointment, Entitlement, Pride, Lust, Greed, Complacency, Doubt, Lies, Worry, Deceit, Guilt, Fear, Jealousy, Manipulation, Unbelief, Mistrust...name your lack? After you have named it, begin to take control and speak the words of Life into every situation.

Speak the Word of God, Believe God's Word. Act on what God has said, and live by the Word of God.

Let's come to understand spiritual death. We know as Christians that we will never die – absent from the body simply means present with the Lord. That's why spiritual death is something that has been vexing my spirit as I minister to women who just do not function in the fullest according to the Word of God.

That's why our mission for this organization emphasizes empowerment – striving to reach our full potential and celebrate life to God's fullest. Many of us are not living to our fullest. We are not realizing our access to God or using the power He has afforded us. So let's not speak death, let's speak of life, let's begin to tell people "we love you to life instead of we love you to death." Death is something that, as a Christian, we should dwell on only because of the resurrection of Jesus, The Christ. Remember that *He died so we may live!* If you are facing a spiritual death begin to declare, as found in Psalm 118:17, "I shall not die, but live, and declare the works of the Lord" Ask yourself, am I living to die or dying to live?

Moments of Reflection

Jesus took the keys of hell and death, so why are we dying?

What has died in your life spiritually?

How can you perform CPR on these issues to bring them back to life — or to bury them if that is what God would have you do?

**Single Is Not Only a Marital Status, It's Also a Mindset
And This Is Not Just About the Single State**

Most of the women that I share fellowship with are single. Of course there is nothing wrong with married women sharing fellowship with single women, but married women do have other priorities and demands on their time. Often, during these times of fellowship with these beautiful, single Sisters that I adore, they will discuss their burning desire to be married and live a godly life with their chosen mate, their earthly king.

And I struggle with how to minister to their single state in a sensitive way because I have been "ecstatically" married for 17 years. So as I pray for them every day, I often ask God why they aren't married. I ask, what is Your Will for them?

As I continue to pray to make some spiritual sense of their state, my spirit ponders this Scripture: 1 Corinthians 7:32-35 NKJV: *32:* "But I want you to be without care. He who is unmarried cares for the things of the Lord – how he may please the Lord. But he who is married cares about the things of the world – how he may please his wife. There is a difference between a wife and a virgin. The unmarried woman cares about the things of the Lord, that she may be holy both in body and in spirit. But she who is married cares about the things of the world—how she may please her husband. And this I say for your own profit, not that I may put a leash on you, but for what is proper, and that you may serve the Lord without distraction."

And now, in our moments of reflection let's examine these questions.

Moments of Reflection

After reading this Scripture, ask yourself honestly, in your singleness rather in marriage, these seven questions – seven in numerology represents the number of completion:

1. Does God want and have my full attention?

2. Does the single woman have a more focused life toward the things of the Lord?

3. Is it truly possible to balance being in love with God and being in love with an earthly king, a mate?

4. Am I being distracted from God by my desire for marriage?

5. Am I failing to find a mate because I have a single mindset? "Is it all about me and what I want?" The "God bless me and no one else syndrome!"

6. Have you consecrated yourself to the Lord according to Deuteronomy 10:12-13?

7. Have you presented yourself as a living sacrifice to God according to Romans 12:1-2?

Answer all these questions honestly and completely. Remember seven is the number of completion. Take a moment to review where you are in your singleness. Be honest with why you are there. Then pray. Ask God for deliverance from whatever is holding you back from finding that special person ordained for you in life.

And for any married women reading this who may be thinking "this doesn't relate to me," think again. Too often we married women are quick to get comfortable with our mate. We feel "I got him now, there is no turning back". But is that true? Take time to be grateful for your spouse and improve yourself. Your marriage will flourish. Treat him like you did when you first met. Enjoy each other; take care of one another.

I am sure some of my single Sistas would love to find a good man like yours and mine.

Finally, I thank God for my king, my mate Fred Sanders, Sr. But most of all I thank God for a King who saved me from sin and loves me for me. And that's definitely going *Beyond the Veil.*

Acknowledgements

**Blessings to all those who joined me as I worked
to fulfill the vision God gave me
and have this book published.**

Many Blessings and Forever Love to:

Rhonda Mouton Flowers. You took "my baby" and nurtured it for me. I am grateful.

Rosalie Spaniel – Your editing skills are truly a gift from God. Thank you for your sensitivity to what God has placed in words through me.

Ingrid Long – Your cover design is a beauty of expression of what I see *Beyond the Veil* . Thank you for your creativity and for expressing God's love for the assignment He gave to me.

Aja J. Grant – Thank you for gathering all my *Beyond the Veils* into one format so we were able to produce our final product – the book we hold in our hand today.

A LOTT of Sista Love – You keep me on my knees and it's from that position that I can serve you to God's fullest.

To My Family:

To my Boaz, Fredricks Sanders, Sr. – Without your support, love, and understanding of who I am in God, none of this would have ever been possible.

Fredricks, Jr. and Frednesha – Thank you for letting me be me, even when it seems to embarrass you.

Janaé and my beautiful grandchildren, Dante, Janiyah, and Serenity – You are always in my prayers and thoughts.

Notes